curious about

BULL RIDING

BY RACHEL GRACK

AMICUS LEARNING

What are you

curious about?

CHAPTER THREE

Bringing Home the Win

Curious About is published by
Amicus Learning, an imprint of Amicus
P.O. Box 227, Mankato, MN 56002
www.amicuspublishing.us

Editors: Ana Brauer and Megan Siewert
Series Designer: Kathleen Petelinsek
Book Designer and Photo Researcher: Emily Dietz

Library of Congress Cataloging-in-Publication Data
Names: Koestler-Grack, Rachel A., 1973– author.
Title: Curious about bull riding / by Rachel Grack.
Description: Mankato, MN : Curious About is published by Amicus Learning, [2025] | Series: Curious about Rodeo | Includes bibliographical references and index. | Audience: Ages 6–9 years | Audience: Grades 2–3 | Summary: "Learn how cowboys and cowgirls compete in bull riding rodeo events in this question-and-answer book for elementary-aged readers. Includes infographics and back matter to support research skills along with table of contents, glossary, books and websites for further research, and index"— Provided by publisher.
Identifiers: LCCN 2024015014 (print) | LCCN 2024015015 (ebook) | ISBN 9798892000864 (lib bdg) | ISBN 9798892001441 (paperback) | ISBN 9798892002028 (ebook)
Subjects: LCSH: Bull riding—Juvenile literature.
Classification: LCC GV1834.45.B84 K64 2025 (print) | LCC GV1834.45.B84 (ebook) | DDC 791.8/4—dc23/eng/20240506
LC record available at https://lccn.loc.gov/2024015014
LC ebook record available at https://lccn.loc.gov/2024015015

Photo Credits: Alamy Stock Photo/H. Mark Weidman Photography, 9; Getty Images/Christian Petersen, 19, Christopher Morris - Corbis, 2, 15, Cindy Ord, 3, 21, Cyrus McCrimmon, 14, David E. Klutho, 16-17, Elsa, 11 (second from top), 11 (bottom), Helen H. Richardson, 11 (top), 11 (middle), 11 (second from bottom), Mark Brown, 10, SOPA Images, 8, THEPALMER, 13; Pexels/@coldbeer, 2, 6, 7; Shutterstock/gaga.vastard, 22, 23, Jackson Stock Photography, cover, 1, 4–5, Steve Lovegrove, 12; The Noun Project/Daniil Churakov, 22, 23

Printed in China

CHAPTER ONE

What is bull riding?

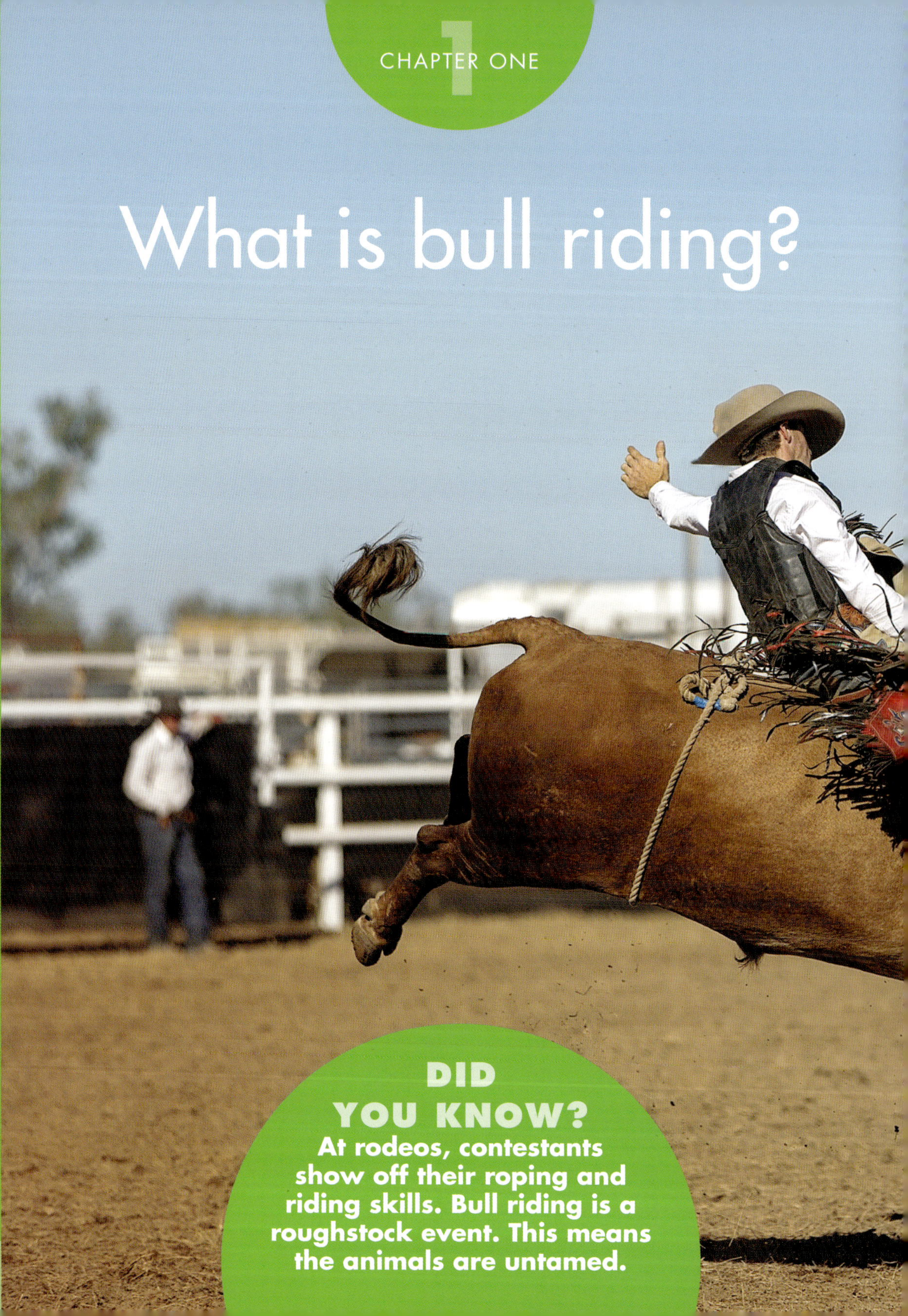

DID YOU KNOW?
At rodeos, contestants show off their roping and riding skills. Bull riding is a roughstock event. This means the animals are untamed.

It's a heart-pounding rodeo sport. A 2,000-pound (907-kilogram) bull waits in the **chute**. It huffs and looks cranky. The contestant climbs on. He wraps a rope around one hand and nods. The bull storms into the arena with powerful kicks, twists, and jumps. Can the cowboy hold on for eight seconds?

Most bull riders compete with the Professional Bull Riders (PBR), the biggest bull riding league in the world.

Bull riders have the risk of getting thrown off or stepped on by the bull.

Is bull riding dangerous?

Extremely. Bull riders take a beating. Just holding on is painful. Riders suffer **dislocated** shoulders. But getting bucked off is worse. Broken bones, torn **muscles**, and **concussions** are common. Plus, riders on the ground become a target. Bulls attack anyone on sight. It can quickly turn deadly. Look out!

A barrelman is a rodeo clown who acts as a barrier between the rider and the bull.

DID YOU KNOW?

Rodeo clowns have a serious job. They keep fallen riders safe by distracting the bull.

Does it take special training?

DID YOU KNOW?
Mutton busting is for kids ages four to seven. They climb on a wild, woolly sheep and hang on as long as they can!

Not really. Riders stay fit and strong. They also need to be lean and quick. Bull riding takes lots of practice, though. Most professional bull riders start when they're young. Some try mutton busting at four years old. At seven, they can begin junior bull riding.

Bull riders train for several hours a day to stay in shape for the sport.

CHAPTER TWO

Do riders wear special gear?

Protective vests became a safety requirement for all bull riders in 1996.

For sure! They all wear leather chaps. These protect their legs. Some events require helmets under a certain age. Safety vests are always required. They lessen the blow if riders get stepped on or hooked by a horn. Riders also wear mouthguards and a glove.

A RIDER'S PROTECTIVE GEAR

1
CHAPS
PREVENTS CUTS AND SCRAPES

2
HELMET
PREVENTS HEAD INJURIES

3
VEST
PROTECTS RIBS AND BACK

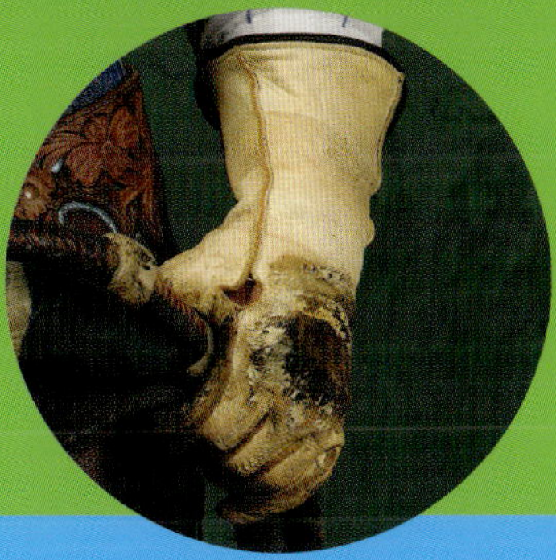

4
GLOVE
PROTECTS HAND FROM ROPE BURN

5
MOUTHGUARD
PROTECTS TEETH AND JAW

A glove gives the rider a better grip on the bull rope.

How do the riders hold on?

WHAT'S WITH THE BELL?

The 8-second buzzer sounds, and the bull rider unties his hand. The weight of the bell causes the bull rope to drop to the ground.

Riders hang on to the bull rope. This is a flat, braided rope tied around the bull's chest. The rider wraps one end of the rope around his hand. Some riders thread it between their fingers. They want a tight hold! Many riders use **rosin** for a better grip.

What makes the bull buck?

Riders use weighted dummies to train bulls to buck.

It's in their blood. Rodeo bulls are **bred** and raised to buck. They start training at a year old. Trainers use bucking dummies to teach them the sport. Bulls learn their job: buck like crazy for eight seconds. Bulls also wear a flank strap. This fleece-lined leather belt gets them to buck even harder.

DID YOU KNOW?

Riders squeeze the bull with their **spurs**. This might make bulls grouchy. But it won't hurt their thick skin. Riders wear dull spurs.

CHAPTER THREE

3

Are there any rules?

If the bull doesn't perform well, the judges can grant the rider a re-ride.

Sure! Riders must last the full eight seconds. Then, a buzzer sounds. Riders who get bucked off sooner get a "no score." But the bull always receives a score. The rider must use just one hand. He cannot touch himself or the bull with his free hand.

What's a good score?

Anything close to 100. Two judges give both the bull and rider a score between zero and 25. Judges rate riders on riding style and body control. Judges score the bull's bucking style and strength. Riders that **spur** the bull for stronger bucks earn more points. The highest score wins.

BULL RIDE SCORING

	BULL: 0–25
JUDGE 1	24
JUDGE 2	23
SCORE	46

DID YOU KNOW?

Wade Leslie is the only bull rider in history to score a perfect 100. He did it in 1991 on a bull named Wolfman.

If the rider isn't thrown off the bull, he dismounts by hopping down.

RIDER: 0–25		POSSIBLE POINTS: 100
22		46/50
23	=	46/50
46		92/100

Why do cowboys ride bulls?

It's a rush! They love the action and thrill. They want a chance to beat the beast. Some professional riders earn big prize money, too. But it takes fearless **grit**. The bull is waiting. Which cowboy has the guts to ride?

Instead of trophies, rodeos award belt buckles to top riders.

ASK MORE QUESTIONS

Who is the best bull rider?

Is there youth bull riding near me?

Try a BIG QUESTION: Could I ride a bull?

SEARCH FOR ANSWERS

Search the library catalog or the Internet. A librarian, teacher, or parent can help you.

Using Keywords
Find the looking glass.

Keywords are the most important words in your question.

If you want to know about:

- the best bull riders, type: FAMOUS BULL RIDERS
- youth bull riding, type: JUNIOR BULL RIDING IN [YOUR STATE]

LEARN MORE

FIND GOOD SOURCES

Here are some good, safe sources you can use in your research. Your librarian can help you find more.

Books

Bull Riding
by Heather Kissock, 2021.

Riding Wild
by Michelle Brown, 2024.

Internet Sites

Britannica Kids: Rodeos
https://kids.britannica.com/students/article/rodeo/276762
Kids Britannica is an encyclopedia with educational information on many topics. Learn more about rodeos.

Wiley Peterson: Bull Rider Coach
https://www.bullridercoach.com/
The Bull Rider Coach website offers information/advice for beginner and experienced bull riders. Find out about upcoming youth bull riding clinics.

Every effort has been made to ensure that these websites are appropriate for children. However, because of the nature of the Internet, it is impossible to guarantee that these sites will remain active indefinitely or that their contents will not be altered.

SHARE AND TAKE ACTION

Watch bull riding.
Ask an adult to help you find bull riding videos.

Try riding a mechanical bull.
Find mechanical bull riding for kids near you.

Attend a bull riding event.
Enjoy eight seconds of heart-thumping action!

GLOSSARY

bred When animals are mated together to produce certain characteristics.

chute A pen that holds animals in position so riders can safely mount.

concussion A serious head injury.

dislocated To get popped out of joint.

grit The ability to keep doing something hard.

muscles Tissue in animals and humans that move parts of the body.

rosin A sticky substance used to improve grip.

spur When cowboys press their spurs against a bull's skin.

spurs The spiked wheels on the heel of a rider's boots.

INDEX

About the Author

Rachel Grack has been writing children's nonfiction for twenty-five years. She lives on a ranch in the heart of rodeo country (southern Arizona). Some evenings, she wanders over to watch her neighbors in friendly roping competitions. A western restaurant in town offers weekly bull riding and mutton busting. But Rachel much prefers a quiet ride on her gentle paint horse, Lady.